HELPFUL PEOPLE

DENTIST

JAMIE FICKETT

NORWOOD HOUSE PRESS

Library of Congress Cataloging-in-Publication Data:

Names: Fickett, Jamie.
Title: Dentist / Jamie Fickett.
Description: Buffalo, NY : Norwood House Press, 2025. | Series: Helpful people | Includes glossary and index.
Identifiers: ISBN 9781684502950 (pbk.) | ISBN 9781684502967 (library bound) | ISBN 9781684502974 (ebook)
Subjects: LCSH: Dentists--Juvenile literature. | Dentistry--Juvenile literature.
Classification: LCC RK63.F535 2025 | DDC 617.6'0232--dc23

Published in 2025 by
Norwood House Press
2544 Clinton Street
Buffalo, NY 14224

Designer: Ocean Books
Editor: Kim Thompson

Photo credits: Cover, p. 1 New Africa/Shutterstock.com; p. 5Media Lens King/Shutterstock.com; pp. 6, 15 Pixel-shot/Shutterstock.com; p. 7 Sergii Kuchugurnyi/Shutterstock.com; p. 9 antoniodiaz/Shutterstock.com; p. 11 DCstudio/Shutterstock.com; p. 12-13 jukov studio/Shutterstock.com; p. 16 Svitlana Hulko/Shutterstock.com; p. 17 Serhii Bobyk/Shutterstock.com; p. 19 Ground Picture/Shutterstock.com; p. 21 Drazen Zigic/Shutterstock.com; p. 23 Dicky Algofari/Shutterstock.com

Printed in the United States of America

CPSIA compliance information: Batch #CW25NHP: For further information contact Norwood House Press at 1-800-237-9932.

TABLE OF CONTENTS

WHAT IS A DENTIST?

Dentists are important helpers in our **community**. Dentists are doctors who take care of our teeth and gums. They help keep our mouths healthy.

Dentists teach us how to brush and floss our teeth. They show us the best way to get rid of all the food and germs in our mouths.

When we have a **cavity**, the dentist will fix it. They fill the cavity hole with a special material.

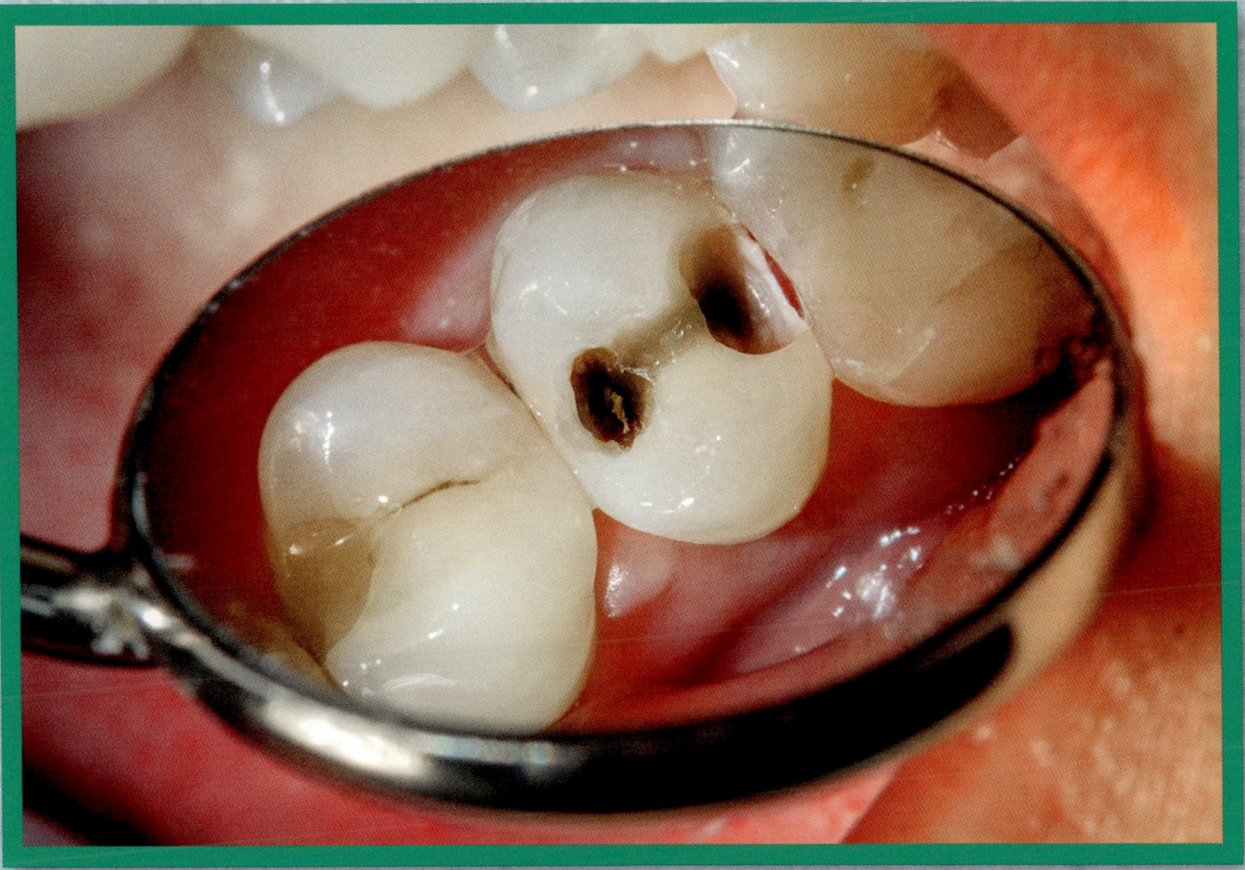

Dentists can fix crooked teeth or gaps between teeth. They put on braces that slowly make the teeth straight.

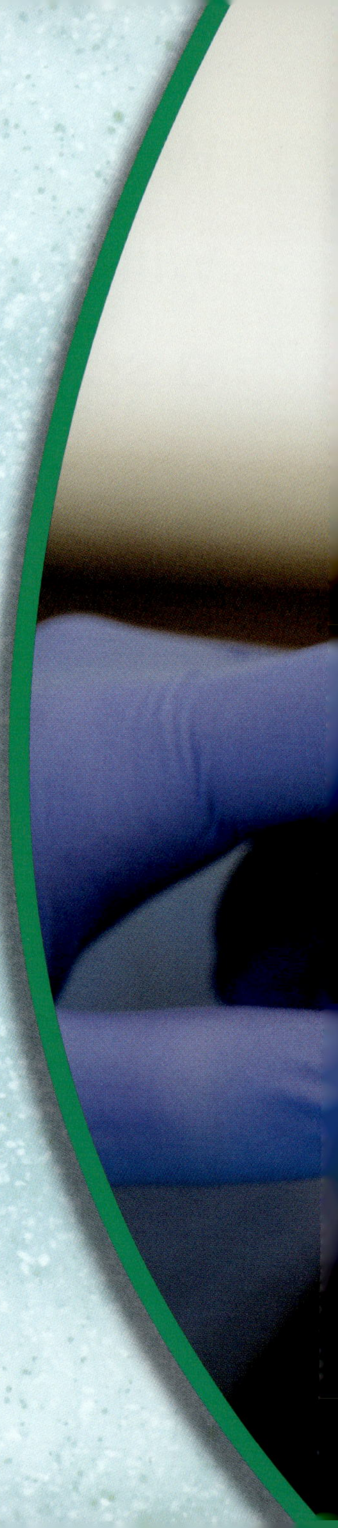

WHAT DOES A DENTIST WEAR?

Many dentists wear a **uniform**. They wear a white lab coat to help keep them clean. They might wear comfortable clothes underneath.

Dentists often wear masks that cover their noses and mouths. They wear clear face shields to **protect** their eyes.

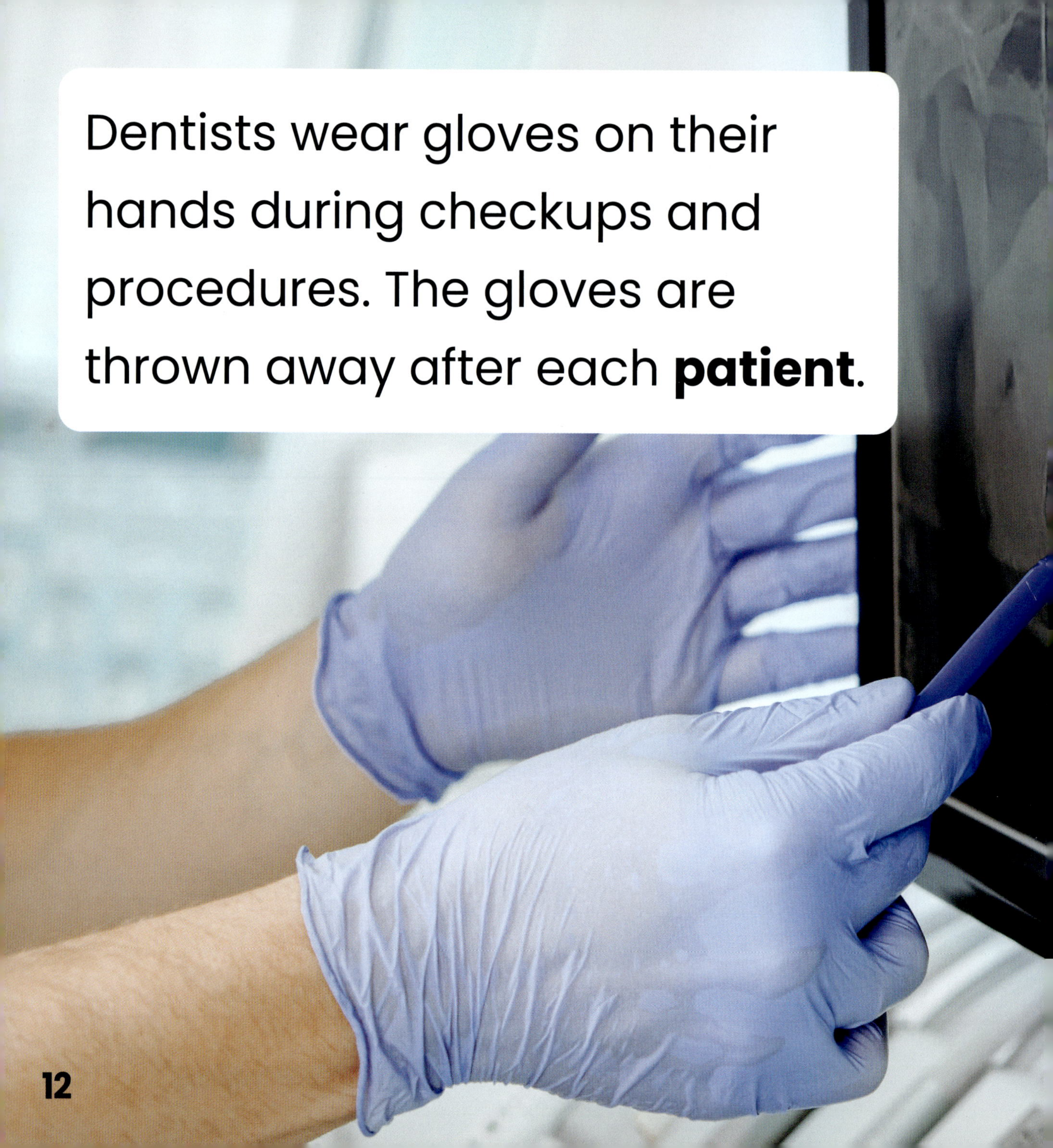

Dentists wear gloves on their hands during checkups and procedures. The gloves are thrown away after each **patient**.

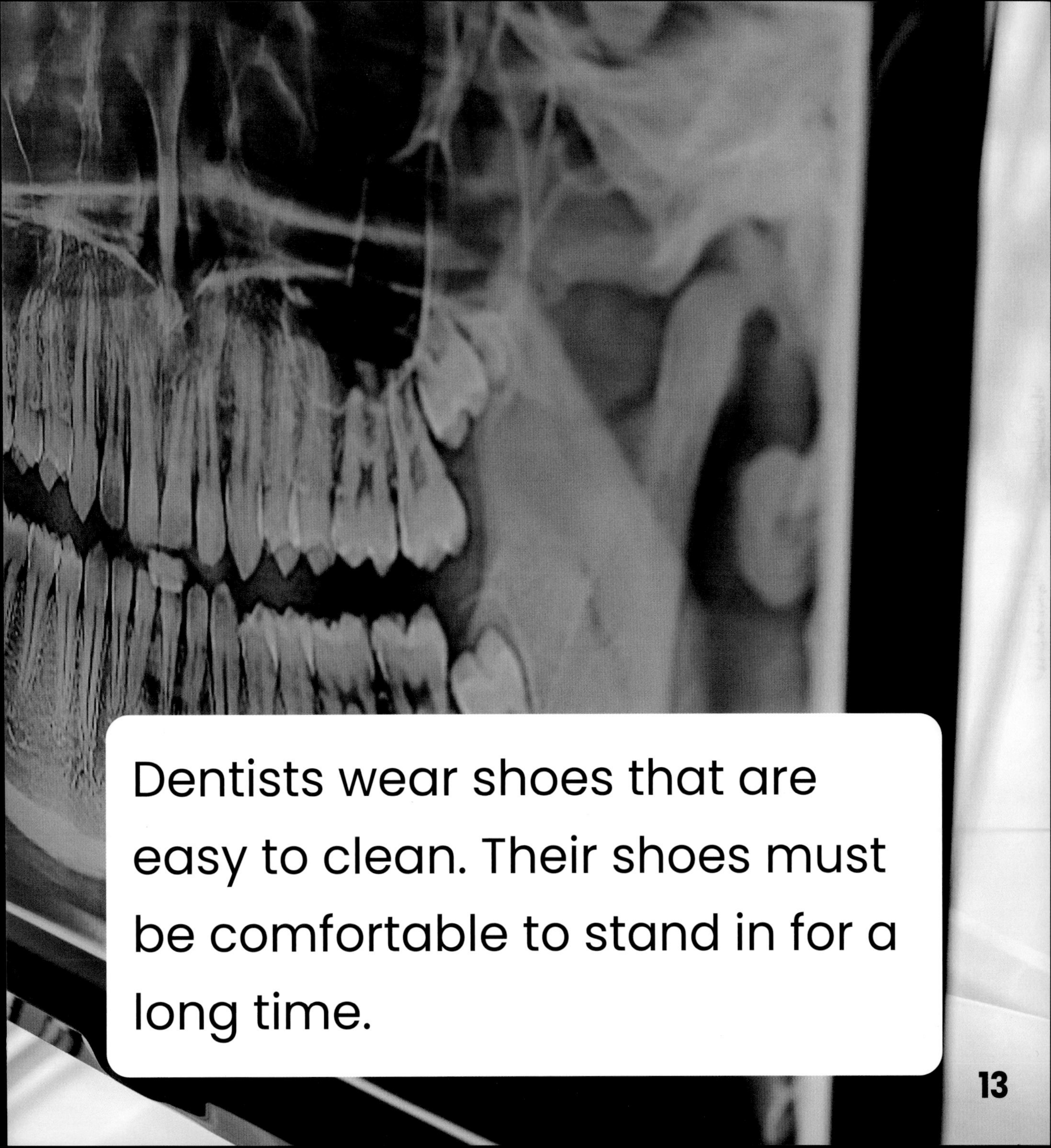

Dentists wear shoes that are easy to clean. Their shoes must be comfortable to stand in for a long time.

WHAT TOOLS DOES A DENTIST USE?

Dentists use **tools** to take care of our teeth. A small mirror helps them see all around inside our mouths. A probe is used to check the health of our teeth and gums.

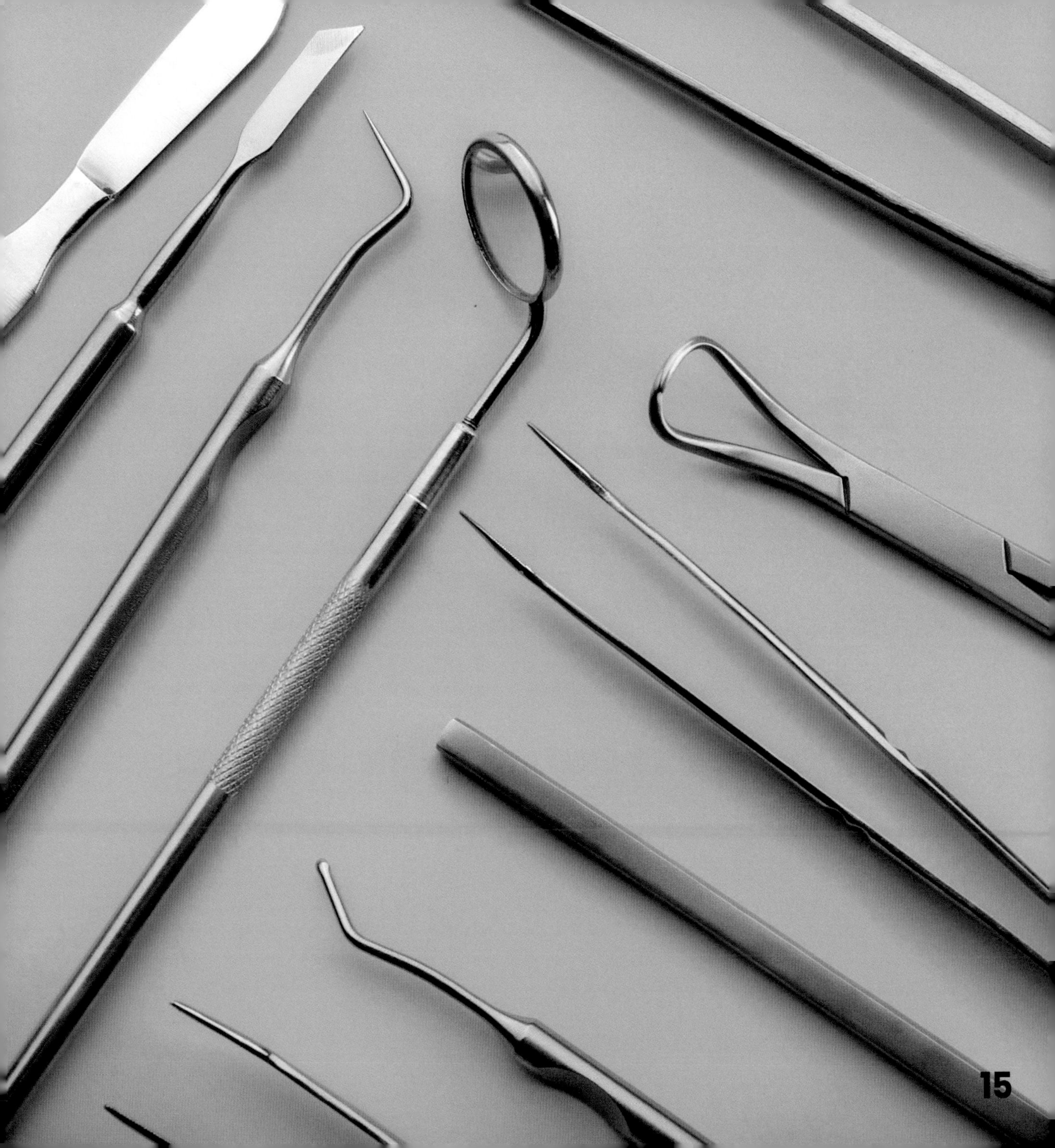

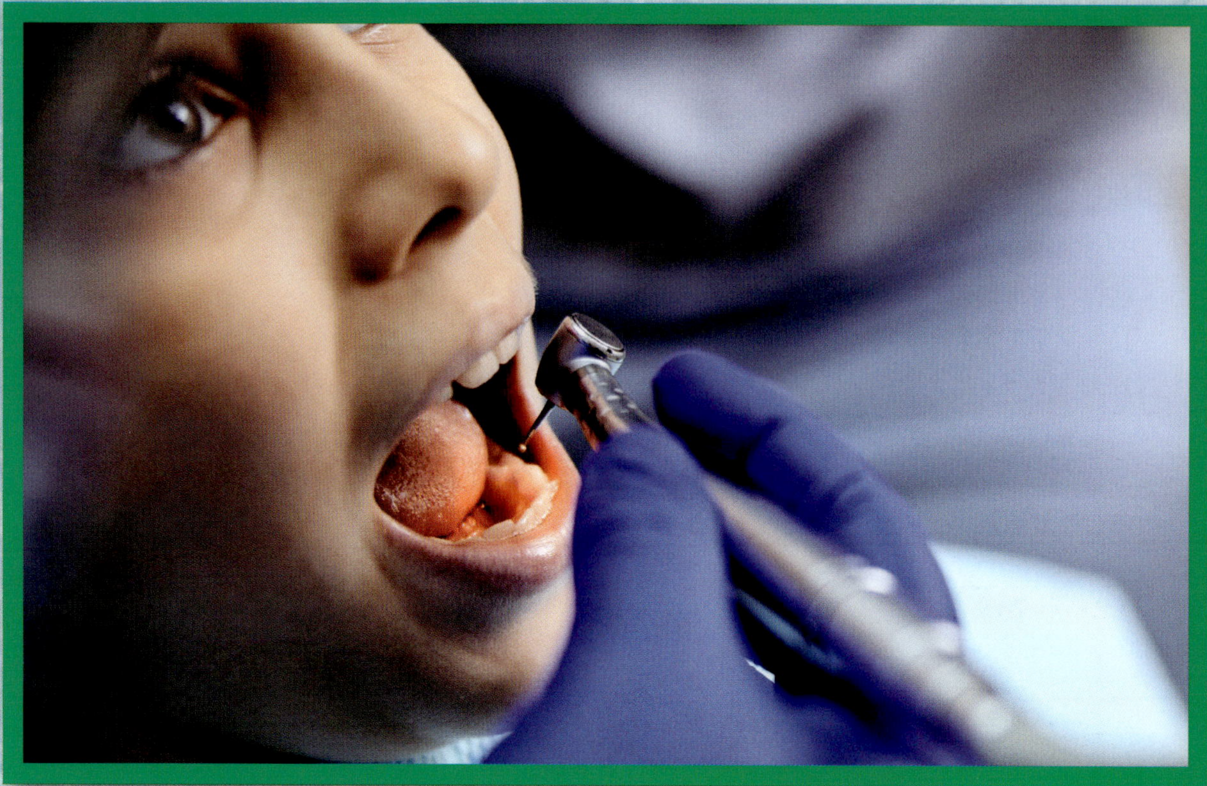

Dentists use a dental drill to clean out the bad parts of our teeth. They make sure to use it gently so it does not hurt.

A scaler scrapes away **plaque** and tartar that can build up and cause gum disease. Dentists make our teeth shiny and smooth by polishing them with a soft brush and special toothpaste.

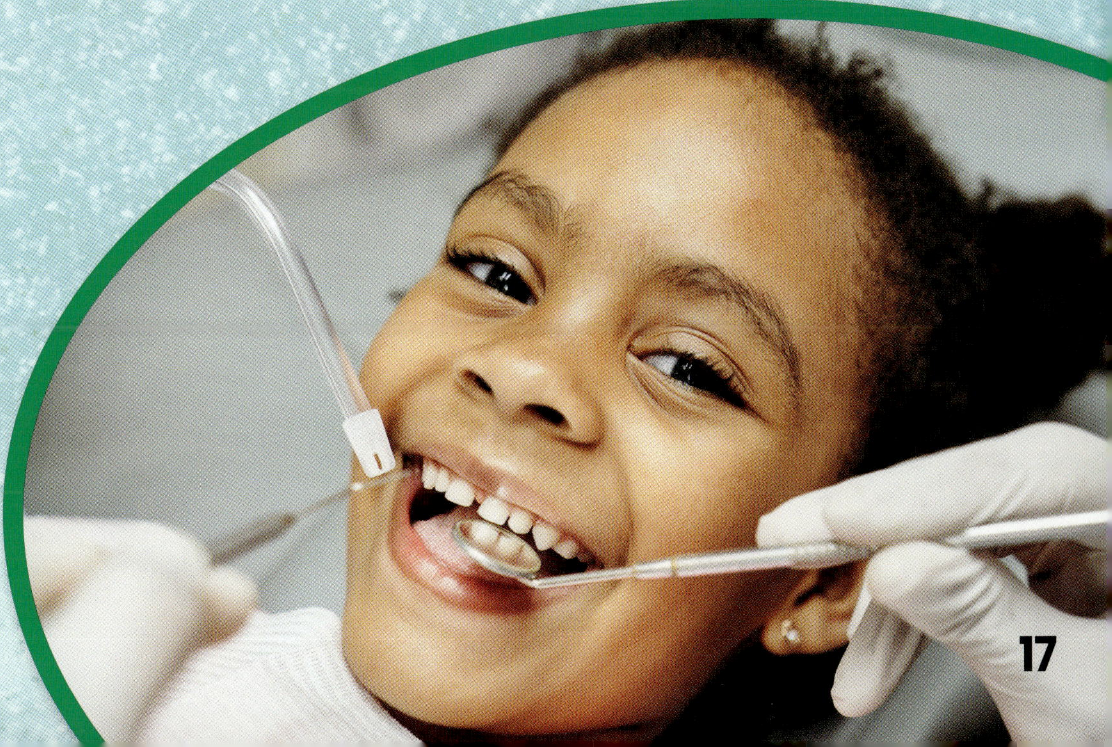

HOW DO YOU BECOME A DENTIST?

To become a dentist, you must finish high school and college. You take a lot of science classes.

Dental school is where you learn how to be a dentist. You get to practice on fake teeth.

Good dentists are caring and gentle when they check our teeth. They need **steady** hands to do their work carefully. They help keep our teeth clean and healthy.

GLOSSARY

cavity (KAV-i-tee): a hollow space or a pit in a tooth

community (kuh-MYOO-ni-tee): a social group of any size whose members live together, have a common government, and often share the same culture or history

patient (PAY-shuhnt): a person who is being treated by a medical professional

plaque (plak): a soft, sticky, whitish, mat-like film that attaches to tooth surfaces and that is usually formed by the growth of bacteria on teeth

protect (pruh-TEKT): to guard and keep safe from harm, attack, injury, or danger

steady (STED-ee): even or regular in movement; not shaky

tools (toolz): pieces of equipment that you use to do a job; things that help you reach a goal

uniform (YOO-nuh-form): a special set of clothes worn by all members of a profession, organization, or rank

THINKING QUESTIONS

1. What is the job of a dentist?
2. Why does a dentist wear gloves?
3. How is a dentist helpful to the community?
4. What are the characteristics of a good dentist?
5. Would you like to become a dentist? Why or why not?

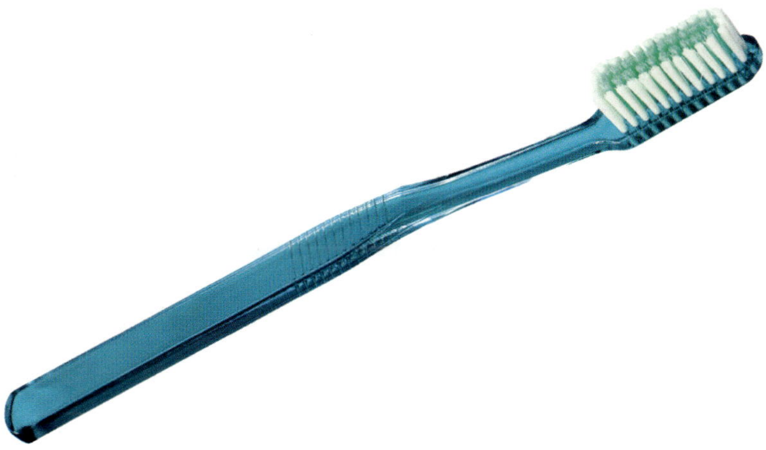

INDEX

ABOUT THE AUTHOR

Jamie Fickett lives on Long Island, New York, where he grew up. Every Saturday he enjoys going to the Bronx Zoo and seeing the rhinos from the Wild Asia Monorail. Rhinoceroses have been his favorite animal ever since he was eight and received the nickname Rhino while playing catcher in Little League baseball.